Great expectations

*A pastoral guide for partnering with parents
to help form their own children in faith*

for catechists and teachers,
pastors, principals,
and parish catechetical leaders

BILL HUEBSCH

with **Leisa Anslinger**

Great expectations

A pastoral guide for **partnering with parents**

For **Catechists**
and **Teachers**,
Pastors,
Principals
and **Parish**
Catechetical
Leaders

TWENTY THIRD *23rd*
PUBLICATIONS
www.23rdpublications.com

ACKNOWLEDGMENTS

We acknowledge with gratitude and respect the Gallup research on parishioner engagement, reported in detail in *Growing an Engaged Church* by Albert L. Winseman, New York, NY, Gallup Press, 2007.

We are also indebted to parishes across the United States, Canada, and United Kingdom who served as sites where we tested the concepts and resources which are reflected in this pastoral guide. Likewise, we are grateful to the many parents and children who voluntarily took part in the early trials.

TWENTY-THIRD PUBLICATIONS
A Division of Bayard
One Montauk Avenue, Suite 200
New London, CT 06320
(860) 437-3012 or (800) 321-0411
www.23rdpublications.com

ISBN 978-1-58595-752-1
Library of Congress Catalog Card Number: 2009926112
Printed in the U.S.A.

CONTENTS

DOWNLOAD AVAILABLE: *Download a FREE parish workshop-retreat to help you launch* **Partnering with Parents** *in your parish. This workshop-retreat lives up to its name. On one hand, it provides you with the PowerPoint and handouts to demonstrate coaching materials and helps parents understand what is expected of them. On the other, it provides a lovely prayer and reflection period to help them see how they are being called to be the primary ones responsible for helping their children to grow up Catholic.*

For more resources and assistance visit

www.PastoralPlanning.com/partnership-parents.html

INTRODUCTION

For catechists and teachers

What do you expect of the parents who have children in your religious ed program or Catholic school? How great are your expectations for their participation in the faith formation of their own children?

The work you do to teach and form young children in the faith—and the expectations we have of their parents—is the subject of this book. We know you prepare well for your classes and provide clear, interesting lessons to the children under your care. We know you spend a good deal of your own money to purchase supplies and teaching tools. We know you make many personal sacrifices on behalf of your class of children.

And we know that those children come to you from homes where the faith you try to pass on to them must be lived. Sometimes the home supports what you do and sometimes it does not. In the cases where the household members

really live their faith at home and the parish, your work is easy. You have only a small gap to fill. You need only help those children deepen their understanding and learn the vocabulary and practices of our faith.

But in those other homes, the ones where the household members are not deeply engaged with their own faith or the parish, your work is much more difficult. With those children, you have a much bigger gap to fill, helping them appreciate Catholic life and culture, Catholic rites and prayer, without the benefit of strong parental support. This is a nearly impossible task!

For we know that faith is passed from adult to child by example and lived experience, not by mere words or textbooks. Children from those active households have a much better chance of growing up Catholic. Even if they wander away for a while during young adulthood, many do return as they settle into their own adult family lives. Of these more active parents, your expectations may be quite high, and reasonably so. They tend to be present at Sunday Mass, active in the parish, and talking about faith at home.

For the children living in households that are disengaged from parish life, even though you do a marvelous job with them, their chances of growing up Catholic are much more slim. The expectations that you have of those parents may be quite low. You may expect them merely to deliver their children to the church or school door for class. You hope they will reinforce what you teach at home, but you know that may not be happening. You do expect them to be present for key turning points such as sacramental celebrations, but even this seems a burden to some of them. Other than that, you may not expect too much of them. And that's our point here. We want you to develop truly great expectations for the parents of your children. We want to help you create a way for them to meet those greater expectations.

In one neighborhood I know, the parish is located near a K-Mart store. Each Wednesday night for many years, this parish held CCD classes for the elementary children. The K-Mart, seeing this, began to advertise "CCD Night Specials" by tucking fliers under the windshield wipers of the cars during Sunday Mass. They knew the parents would deposit their children at the parish church and go shopping. Smart marketing, but sad news for the parish.

A change in course

This manual, we hope, will help you prepare for a course change in how we approach our families. We want to shift our approach in order to include both active and inactive parents or guardians in the formation of their own children. We want to build this new approach on your dedication, skills, and devotion to your ministry as a teacher or catechist, whether in a Catholic school or parish program.

At first, any change in course seems confusing and disorienting to people who have long followed one, well-known method. But we know this change will pay off well! We know that if you can help include those parents and guardians in the learning cycle of their children, tremendous fruit will grow on the branches of our parish or school religion class tree.

What do we want of you?

We would like you to learn with us how to help parents take on the role of the primary religion teacher of their own children. Believe it or not, this will actually make your work much easier. And it will also make your work much more fulfilling because you will see firsthand the great hope that rises up as parents become involved in this way. This great hope becomes obvious early in the process of this new approach.

For it turns out that parents really do want to be involved in their children's faith lives. They want to be able to speak to their own children about God, about religious matters, about morals and values, and about the social teachings of the Church. They want to, but even for those who are active in the parish, most do not know how. They feel inadequate and unqualified.

And this is where you come in, for you are very qualified and you can assist them to become more capable and confident. You can help them find the vocabulary and help them see how important their own example of faith is to their children. You can guide them gently, letting them teach and form their child.

You might be wondering at this point how you could ever do this. You can do it by becoming their coach. A basketball coach is not the ball player. Rather, working from the sidelines, coaches lead the actual players to learn the methods and play them out on the court. If you think of yourself as a coach like this, you shift from being the main player to coaching the parents so that they can become the main players. You work from the sidelines now and they carry out the work of teaching and forming.

What do you need to succeed?

Well, first of all, you need those parents to be in the room with their children during at least some portions of the religious education process. They may not need to be present at every moment in every class, but at certain key points along the way, you need them to be there.

This is not your worry as a teacher or catechist. This job belongs to your principal or religion program director. It belongs to the pastor and committee members in your parish or school who do the planning. It's rather nice that you don't have to worry about this, isn't it? (And if you're the principal, director, pastor, or

Parents really do want to be involved in their children's faith lives.... They want to, but even for those who are active in the parish, **most do not know how.**

committee member in question, the next section of this manual is for you.)

Second, you do need a resource to give the parents to help them. The resource should be parent-friendly and easy to follow. It should have clear steps for them to take, clear lines of thought, and all the answers to any activities in which their children might engage as part of the lesson. We're going to show you an example of such "parent coaching notes" a bit later, but for now, please know that you do not have to invent these notes. You may eventually have a hand in creating new ones for your parents, but to get you started, we are providing them for you.

Third, you need certain skills and knowledge about what it means to coach parents to form their own children. This manual provides you with a short course in just that sort of thing. But practice also makes perfect. You will learn much of what you need to know by actually working with the parent coaching notes. We also provide you with a lovely set of your own notes, as a catechist or teacher, to help you become a superb coach yourself.

Fourth—and this is true whether you remain a religion teacher or catechist, or become a parent coach—you need faith. God is working in your own life as well as in the lives of your young learners. I know this is sometimes hard to believe when they are disruptive, rowdy, or antsy in your classroom or other faith formation setting. Our task is really to help them see that God is present, and then to help them comprehend the meaning of that through religion class or catechesis, to help them celebrate with awe in liturgy and prayer, and to help them shape a lifestyle of faith that reflects the teachings of the Master Teacher himself, Jesus Christ.

How do you get started as a coach?

The first thing we want you to do is to read the rest of this pastoral guide. If possible, we would like to see you spend a day together with other teachers, catechists, your principals and directors, pastors and leaders. Spend this day reading this pastoral guide together. Pause at the end of each section and talk about the main points, using the framework we provide for you.

The second thing we want you to do is to follow the lead of your parish director or coordinator of religious education or your school principal and religion department head. The very next section of this Introduction is addressed to them, but we'd like for you to read it as well. It will help you come to understand more fully your new role in this exciting new moment of religious education history.

INTRODUCTION

For pastors, principals, and catechetical leaders

If you just read our message to the catechists and teachers who work under your leadership, then you already can guess what might be asked of you. To bring parents into the learning circle of your program is not as difficult as it sounds. But we have tried and failed to do so in the past, so some of us may feel reluctant to try again, even though we agree with the central premise, which is that we cannot succeed with their children unless we do bring them into the process. Like the catechists and teachers we addressed above, we also want to encourage you to have far greater expectations of the parents and guardians who have children in your programs.

In recent years, we have tried this or that...

We have sometimes gathered parents with their children and done intergenerational formation events. We have sometimes asked the parents to take home the book and actually do the faith formation themselves. We have sometimes asked the parents to meet as adults while their children were in religion class. Most of the time, we have been willing to substitute our catechists and teachers for the parents, allowing the parents to be absent while their children are in class.

...But we have not offered to coach the parents to form their own children. This is the key. When we do coach parents with a friendly resource and good process, they actually love it. In parish after parish where such a method is being used, parents report wanting more, not less. They gain confidence. They become involved. They learn the answers. They are evangelized and reengaged.

But—and here is the secret to this—we succeed at this only when we meet them where they are in life and faith. By this I mean that we accept where they're at in terms of faith experience and abilities. We can't unravel every complex marriage case before we invite them. We can't sort out all their doubts and issues with the Church first. We can't send them into training as catechists or mini-theologians. Rather, we must trust and gently urge them to follow the coaching notes (which are aimed almost more at them than their children) and let this be the starting point.

We have learned that, when we do this, we can indeed have great expectations of our parents and guardians, and they will meet them. They will rise to the occasion and come to play the principal role in the education of their children in faith.

This pastoral guide is designed to be used by you as leaders, along with your catechists and teachers. Read it together and spend a day or two reflecting on the various elements of this process.

Chapter One: Why Parents Are So Important in Faith Formation introduces this concept in more detail, giving a brief history of the cultural setting in which we all work today in the United Kingdom, United States, Canada, Ireland, and Australia. This chapter lays out plainly what new, great expectations we want to create for the parents of our children, to evangelize and form the parents, and to do so with their children.

Chapter Two: The Parents and the Parish continues exploring the concept and gives the key principles we want to follow. Here we study short excerpts from the *General Directory for Catechesis* (a key document from the Vatican that guides all religious education or cateche-

When we coach parents with a friendly resource and good process, they actually love it.…They gain confidence. They become involved. They learn the answers. They are evangelized and reengaged.

sis throughout the world). In this chapter, we also introduce some examples of parent coaching notes. This important chapter also explains the Catholic ecclesiology that lies at the base of this method.

Chapter Three: A Plan to Help Children Grow Up Catholic traces the outline of a parish organizational plan aimed at coaching parents, beginning with the baptism of their child and continuing until that child is a young adult and out of secondary school.

Chapter Four: What Coaching Is and What It Is Not opens up a discussion about the process and the skills needed to succeed at it. Understanding what it means to coach—instead of teach—is essential.

Chapter Five: Getting Started in Your Parish helps you see how you can add this method to your current programs for

- Sacrament prep for reconciliation and Holy Communion, plus confirmation in restored order
- Confirmation programs for students in junior or senior high school
- Your basal curriculum in your Catholic school or parish religious education program.

In Chapter Four, we also lay out the process for getting started with all of this in your parish.

Appendix: An example of a resource designed to coach parents for the preparation of their children for first Eucharist, taken from *Growing Up Catholic.* Coaching notes such as these could be drawn up for any textbook lesson.

CHAPTER ONE

Why parents are so important in faith formation

Much current research and a great deal of anecdotal evidence supports the premise that most adult Catholics are active in the Church today because they were formed in faith by their own parents. Of course, some adults do come to the Church as adults. And, of course, many adults whose parents took great care to form them have drifted away from the regular practice of their faith.

Nevertheless, most adult Catholics remain active in their faith because they were formed by their parents. This is *faith formation that lasts a lifetime!* It does not end with primary school.

Study after study highlights the importance of this. People experience less difficulty with drug and alcohol abuse, depression and suicide, and family tension when they regularly come to church; children and teens are more likely to do well in school, stay close to their families, and experience a greater sense of well-being when they regularly participate in Mass and parish activities with their families. Yet, as Church historian Scott Appleby notes,

No previous generation of American Catholics has inherited so little of the content and sensibility of the faith from their parents, as have today's Catholic youth. The challenge of Catholic education and formation in our media-driven, cyberspace age is no less than this: older Catholics must be restored to, and younger Catholics introduced to, a sense of Catholicism as a comprehensive way of life.

From a speech he gave on October 16, 2002 to the Catholic Academy for Communications Arts Professionals

In other words, we must now help our children to grow up Catholic in new and more effective ways.

The fact is that we cannot substitute anyone else for the work of faith formation. Parents are the key players. This is Principle One. They are forming their children whether they practice their faith or not. If they are active in their faith, their children see faith in them and see in that a "hidden message" that faith is important and that we are responding to God's call when we respond in faith. If they are not active, their children see a "hidden message" in that as well: that faith is not very important in daily life and that it is optional.

This latter belief, that faith is something optional that we can choose or not, lies at the heart of the challenge for us. In fact, faith is a response we make to God revealing God's self to us in many, fascinating ways. It's a response, more than a choice. The response we make arises within us when we yield to the power of the Holy Spirit. Within each human person is a great, mysterious force—the force and power of love—which is where God touches our hearts and sets us free.

When we yield to it and respond, we find ourselves falling headlong into the teachings of Jesus: forgiveness, generosity, hospitality, shared meals, community life, commitments of love, and general beatitudinal living. The more we yield to this, the more we live in that loving, divine power.

The Church helps us do this in ways that cannot be replaced by any other agency in the world. It makes sacramental the daily experience of forgiveness, shared meals, and love. It provides the community context in which faith is nurtured and formed. For those who

We cannot substitute anyone else for the work of faith formation. **Parents are the key players.**

are called to be Catholic, the Church, indeed, is necessary for healing, wholeness, and all things salvific.

. . . .

PRINCIPLE ONE:
We cannot succeed in faith formation with children unless their parents are also deeply engaged with the process.

. . . .

Cultivating deep communion with Christ is the journey of each Christian, each Catholic. Such deep communion is "of the heart" more than "of the head."

Faith, therefore, is not something to be "understood" as much as something to be "lived." You can't learn to live faith in a classroom setting alone. You can't learn it in any sort of CCD, religious education, faith formation, or school setting alone. What happens in those settings is important, but it only works when faith is being lived *outside* of those settings.

Faith is lived

This key idea helps us understand why parents are so vital in the formation of children. And until very recently parents have always been the key players in that formation. They have created homes in which love and charity were paramount, homes in which the feasts and seasons of the liturgical year were the backbone, homes in which God-talk was common. Formation was household-centered.

Take a look at this chart, which explains how we shifted away from household-centered formation in the United States, England, Canada, and other western nations.

TIME PERIOD	WHAT HAPPENED
From 1910 or so up to the 1950s	Catholic life lived in households, but in isolation from the culture.
	Catholic children learned about their faith by living in a household of faith. The members of this household attended Mass every week and prayed at home: before every meal, every morning and evening, and together as a family especially during Lent, by fasting, abstaining, setting up Marian altars, and observing feasts and seasons. They carried holy cards in their pockets, glued statues of saints to their dashboards, and generally lived their faith day in and day out.
	CCD class or Catholic school filled in a tiny gap in the formation process. It offered the formulas and definitions, the doctrine and dogma, needed to elaborate the experience of faith which was going on in daily life. Catholic school religion or parish CCD class used a small catechism as its main source, but was greatly expanded by the sisters and brothers who did most of the teaching.
	The example of faith coming from the religious sisters and brothers who did the teaching was an enormous factor. But it remains true that it was the "Catholic home life" from which the children came that formed the bedrock of faith.
In the 1960s **Vatican II**	Major cultural shift in the western world. The breakdown of the solid Catholic life.
	The culture of Catholic home life began to change as transportation, communication, and media emerged with great force. The old piety of the 1950s gave way at home to television, out-of-home activities, TV dinners, and the influence of movements for social change.
	Families prayed together less, and lived a less explicit Catholic piety.
	The CCD or Catholic school now had a much larger gap to fill. There was less in-home formation, and parents now began to feel freer to embrace the social change of the culture. This meant more ecumenical marriages, less regular attendance at Sunday Mass, fewer children per family, less formal obedience to Church teaching, and greater openness to other faiths.
	Religion class generally no longer used the old catechism, but also had not found anything new. It used pop culture itself as a means of teaching the faith: music, crafts, and "faith experiences" of various kinds, including experimental methods for faith formation.

TIME PERIOD	WHAT HAPPENED
In the 1970s and beyond **Catholic home life all but disappears**	The practice of faith had increasingly less influence on home life. Unlike the 1950s, there was now almost no practice of faith at home: fasting, abstaining, and family prayer were a thing of the past, by and large.
	CCD or schools shifted to actual textbooks in order to fill in the huge chasm that now existed between daily life and faith. The role of parents was reduced to almost nothing. Home life had very little God-talk going on in it. Parents got into the habit of depositing their children at parish centers where non-family members (i.e., parish catechists or school teachers) now taught them about religion.
In the 1980s and '90s *On Catechesis Today* **The restoration of the catechumenate (or RCIA)**	The engagement of adult Catholics with the Church continues to decline. Children continue to be taught religion by volunteers at the parish, rather than by their parents. This made faith more cognitive than emotive for many.
	The practices of religious education became entrenched in parish life, with major textbook series being published to support it. Parents remained at the fringe of this, except for a slowly emerging movement to include them in preparation for confession and first Communion.
	Meanwhile, the popes, bishops, and academic circles within the Church were rethinking faith formation. A reform emerged from this that was rooted, not in a return to the 1950s, but in a return to the very first centuries of the Church. The process through which people prepared to be initiated into the Church at baptism was restored. That process is called the catechumenate. It was seen as the new basis for ALL faith formation.
In the new millennium and up to the present day **Whole community catechesis** **Lifelong faith formation** **Coaching parents to form their own children**	The engagement of adult Catholics with the Church continues to decline. Children continue to be taught their religion by volunteers at the parish, rather than by their parents.
	But as the reform launched in the last decade took hold, several new dimensions to faith formation emerged. First and foremost among them is that conversion to Christ was seen as central to all formation. Knowing the person of Christ and having communion with him took center stage. "Conversion," the GDC says (#62), "precedes catechesis."
	Second is the reemergence of the understanding that parents are indeed the ones primarily responsible for forming their own children in faith. No parish volunteers or school teachers, no matter how well meaning and talented, can substitute for parents. This called on us to re-develop a Catholic home life, but under modern terms. (GDC #255)
	Third is the clear understanding that formation in faith is lifelong. It does not end when primary school ends (GDC #176 et al.). We are now being called upon to provide formation for adults at every age and stage of life.

Where is this leading us?

If you consider the three main elements in the reform of faith formation now going on:

- that it is Christ-centered
- that it depends on parents
- that it is lifelong

we can begin to see the pathway forward. This new pathway is one that affects you as a volunteer catechist, school teacher, or parish leader.

We must all be careful not to continue using a method for Catholic school religion programs, and parish CCD, religious education, or faith formation that seems not to be working. We can't keep hoping for a better outcome next year than we had last year. We can see in our own studies and reports that the level of engagement for adult Catholics continues to decline, and we believe this is because we have not engaged parents deeply enough in the formation of their own children. We really have not engaged people deeply enough in the life of Christ through the community of faith, the parish.

Research tells us that engagement is a deep sense of belonging within the parish that makes a remarkable difference in the way people live their faith. This belonging is a relationship among people, and, through it, people know Christ's love; they sense the importance of being rooted in the community when they encounter difficulties in life and when they have something wonderful to celebrate. When people are engaged, they know the parish values each person as a child of God. People who are engaged are more likely to invite others to come with them to church; they serve in their parishes and in their local town; they give of their financial resources; they are more satisfied in their lives.

In other words, being engaged is really important, and what better time to help people become engaged than when their children are young, when we know that we will touch the whole family? Parents who see the parish as a community of people who care for each other will grow in their faith and the way their faith guides and directs their lives.

Every relationship has expectations, doesn't it? Our relationship with the parish is no different. In parish life we need to be clear about what we expect of one another, because that will help each person to grow in their sense of belonging, of being of value within the parish. Early in the process of engagement, of helping people to develop that important sense of belonging, people need to know what is expected of them, and they need to sense that their spiritual needs will be met.

Reading through the chart above, it might have already become obvious to you that we Catholic leaders must have *great expectations* of our parents, if we hope to succeed at any form of children's religious education and formation. Hence the title of this book.

As parish leaders and volunteer catechists or school religion teachers, we now understand that we really aren't the ones who do the primary faith formation of the children in our classes. Their parents play that role. We play a secondary role to reinforce and support the work of the parents. For most of us, this turns around how we have been thinking about our ministry. In the past and for many of us, still today, we see ourselves often as the *primary teachers* of the children, with their parents playing the role of reinforcement.

What would a parish or school religion class look like under these new terms? This is where parish leaders and volunteers must work closely together. We know that many of the parents with children in our faith formation programs and schools are not themselves very engaged in parish life. The statistics tell us that only about sixteen percent of Catholics are engaged in their parishes. Most are not engaged. They don't come to Mass on Sundays very often. They don't contribute much money to support the parish. They live on the fringe of parish life—for the most part.

There may be some good reasons for this in their lives. They might be divorced, or remarried without an annulment. They might be married to a non-Catholic who fights the intrusion of religion into household life. They might have a past of which they are too ashamed to make amends, to return to confession and Communion. Who knows? People go through a lot in life, and many times it isn't according to Church norms.

There really are two groups of parents in every parish. There's that one group we just described, which is minimally engaged. But there is also the other group of parents, smaller but stronger, that is very engaged in the parish. These people do come to Mass on a regular basis. They do contribute money to support the parish. And they do take an active role in their children's formation. They serve on parish committees and councils. And they would love to see more people actively engaged.

But whatever their reasons for being mainly unengaged, the parents in that first group do have an inner hunger for more vigor in their faith life. They dearly want their children to grow up in the faith they hold. Even if they aren't engaged, when you ask them, they tell you they're still Catholic. It's important to them in a deep way, and were it not so frightening for them, they would become more active themselves.

And here's the key thing we have learned: When coached to do so, these parents, like the more engaged ones, do indeed take on the primary role in the formation of their children.

In this book, we will introduce you to a method for your classroom or faith formation setting in which catechists play that secondary role (the coach) and the parents play the primary role (the teachers). As a parish leader, you'll be amazed at how fulfilling it is to assist the parents as they step up to form their own children. And in both cases—that of the parish leader and that of the religion teacher or catechist—the feedback you get from the parents will be overwhelmingly positive.

In regard to religious education of their children, the expectations we have of the parents are going to become greater and greater. We're going to expect them to take the primary role in forming their own children and in being part of the parish process of faith formation or catechesis.

QUESTIONS FOR DISCUSSION

1. What was your own experience of faith when you were growing up? What or who helped you to develop a lasting faith in Christ and love for the Church?

2. In what ways does your parish already help parents to see their vital role in forming their children in our faith? Do you work in partnership with parents and does that partnership include a clear articulation of the expectations you hold for one another?

3. How does your parish help people feel they belong and are of value within the faith community?

CHAPTER TWO

The parents and the parish

What if, instead of substituting Catholic school teachers or volunteer parish catechists for parents in the formation of children, we coached parents to form their own children, but did so in a parish setting?

In this approach (which is much easier to succeed at than you might think), the current teacher or volunteer catechist becomes the coach. And the currently mostly absent parent or guardian becomes the parent-catechist.

In order for this to work, you'll need a suitable resource, one that takes parents seriously and works with them realistically, taking into account where they currently are in their lives. Parents don't always have the correct terminology (many do but many don't), they may not know the theology, and they may not even be attending liturgy regularly. But—and this is the key point—they are still the parents of those children. With the right resource, they can

learn with their children. And when they do so, they are also "evangelized" by the process itself. Many return to more active status. And most increase the God-talk and faith life of the household.

As background to this, consider our own Church teachings

Who does the *Catechism of the Catholic Church* say should provide spiritual and religious formation for children? That's right: "Parents have the first responsibility for the education of their children" (CCC #2223).

Who does Vatican II say has the responsibility for educating children in the faith? That's right: "The role of parents in education is of such importance that it is almost impossible to provide an adequate substitute" (*Declaration on Christian Education*, #3).

Who does the *General Directory for Catechesis* say is charged with the task of educating children? That's right: "Parents are the primary educators in the faith" (GDC, #255).

There is often a bit of unconscious thinking on the part of parish leaders about this. We see that parents seem unwilling or unable to serve as volunteer catechists at the parish, and we secretly suspect they aren't engaging in much God-talk with their children at home. We see parents and children today as generally overextended, busy, and not fully engaged with the parish.

And yet, we also all believe in the prin-

From the *General Directory for Catechesis*...

[226] The witness of Christian life
  given by parents in the family
  comes to children with tenderness and
    power.
Thus, children grow up, living in the closeness
    of love,
  which is the closeness of God and Jesus,
  made plain by their parents
    and this leaves its mark for the rest
      of their lives!
The childhood religious awakening
  which takes place
  in the family
  is, simply, irreplaceable.
It is most powerful when parents
    take the time
  to explain to their children
  the religious significance or meaning
    of events which occur
    including holy days, family moments,
    and social, political or moral questions.
And this is made even more powerful
  when parents connect it to the

methodical catechesis
  their children receive at the parish program.
Indeed, we might say that "family catechesis
  precedes...accompanies and enriches
    all forms of catechesis."

[227] In the sacrament of matrimony,
  parents receive the grace and the ministry
    of the Christian education of their
      children.
This educational activity,
  which is both human and religious,
  is a true ministry through which the
      Gospel is proclaimed
    and family life is transformed
      into a journey of faith.
The Christian community must, therefore,
  help parents
  by whatever means works best,
  to prepare for and assume their
    responsibility,
    which is especially delicate today,
    of educating their children in the faith.

FROM **THE GDC IN PLAIN ENGLISH** (NEW LONDON, CT: TWENTY-THIRD PUBLICATIONS) *ciple we're defining here:* that we cannot succeed with children unless their parents are in the picture. We all want to provide formation that will last a lifetime, not merely until they're out of school. And we know that to succeed at this, the children must learn in the "school of the household." But we're in the habit of "doing it for parents" and allowing the parents to be absent if they wish. We have moved almost all faith formation to the parish campus and out of the home.

....

PRINCIPLE ONE:
We cannot succeed in faith formation with children unless their parents are also deeply engaged with the process.

....

What we are learning, however, is that if you coach those parents, they not only come forward to get involved, but they want to get involved and they really enjoy the experience. If we coach parents well, all the formation goes home. It goes home in their hearts—and it stays there.

How coaching might work

For example, in preparation for first reconciliation or first Eucharist, convene a new form of catechetical setting. Gather children who are preparing for first Eucharist (Holy Communion) in second grade, for example, along with their parents and guardians, even if some of them are not Catholic. Arrange the room so that each "household group" can sit and work together. If there are children who have no parent or guardian available, then bring in someone from the parish to act as a surrogate—an older student from the youth ministry program, or a willing volunteer or grandparent, for example. The seating can be around the end of the typical parish rectangular table, or around one side of a large round table, or even at smaller tables or desks that fit the children better.

This session will last about fifty-five minutes. The room will be warmly lit (too much fluorescent light never works!), with sacred music playing (the parish leader notes direct you about this), and with all the materials printed and ready to go. An altar will be set up to create a central prayer space in the center of this room for the prayer celebration that is part of every session. During this prayer celebration, the household groups will temporarily leave where they're sitting, leaving all the materials just where they are on the tables, and scrunch together messily around this altar. They'll pray together and then return to their work.

This informal scrunching and prayer breaks the ice for everyone and helps the parents and children see that we can have fun and be "loose" while still doing excellent faith formation.

The catechist will coach a process in which the parents do the teaching and formation, using a resource that enables this. Rather than teaching the children as he or she normally would, the catechist becomes more of a "ring leader."

In a circus, the ring leader keeps many acts

moving at once, helping here and there and spotting problems before they get out of hand. Likewise in the faith formation setting where parents attend with their own children, you'll have multiple sets of households working, each at their own pace, and yet all together in a single forward movement through the lesson. You're the ring leader of this process, and the catechist notes show you how this is done for each session.

We suggest that in some groups, you may wish to make use of additional supervisory persons or "floaters" who roam about the room, keeping an eye on the proceedings and spotting troubled parents before they become too frustrated.

In the end, you are providing an environment where the parents-with-their-children can self-manage their learning. This is at the core of what people need in order to make this work. This is how they will take it home and make it last a lifetime.

> ## From the GDC about the ones being catechized...
>
> [157] Those to be catechized cannot be
>   passive recipients
> but must be actively engaged
>   in the process
> through prayer,
>   participation in the sacraments,
>   the liturgy,
>   parish life
>   social commitments,
>   works of charity,
>   and the promotion of human values.
> Catechesis, after all, is a process of
>   taking on
> a way of life and personal conversion,
> not the acquisition of a body of
>   information.
>
> FROM **THE GDC IN PLAIN ENGLISH**
> (NEW LONDON, CT: TWENTY-THIRD PUBLICATIONS)

Evidence that this really works

Here's some anecdotal evidence to show how well this approach works.

In one parish with sixteen children in preparation for first reconciliation, we divided the class in half. Eight worked with a traditional catechist or religion teacher, who taught from the same text used by the other group. She was a great teacher and followed the lesson plan as outlined in the resource.

The other eight were in the setting where parents were coached to do the formation. Both groups had about fifty-five minutes to complete the lesson. In the second group, the catechist followed the guide, which called for her to coach the parents and keep them on track, but to allow them to do the majority of the work.

In the traditional setting, the catechist read the lesson's Scripture story to the children, who then colored a picture from it. Later, she asked them to retell the story in their own words. Only two (twenty-five percent) were able to do so.

In the group with parents being coached to form their own children, each parent worked through the Scripture story in children's language *with them*, they colored a picture of the story *together*, and then the parent *helped them prepare* to retell the story, and nearly eighty percent could do so! Not only that, but we also know that, for the latter group, the Scripture story and the picture they colored together, *went home with them and stayed there*.

Developmental specialists know that reading aloud to children helps to stimulate brain development, long after the child has become an independent reader. Not only that, children learn through repetition, and they are more likely to remember what they have learned when they believe it has meaning for their lives. So hearing the story from their parents, reflecting on the story through the coloring exercise, and retelling the story in their own words helps the child to recognize the deeper meaning of the stories they hear from sacred Scripture.

Those who are familiar with the Catechesis of the Good Shepherd may recognize similar methodology in what we are suggesting. Drawing on observations of children from an early age, we realize that children have within them a deeply imbedded desire and need for a relationship with God that is expressed in wonder and joy. That relationship is echoed and made visible through the child's relationship with his or her parents, expressed through moments such as the ones we will offer around the table at the parish, as an expression of the Body of Christ.

It's just better formation to have the parents in the picture like this, and feedback from the parents is universally positive. The coaching is not condescending, nor does it demand of them that they become mini-theologians. It respects them as parents, understanding that they themselves may not have had any formation since their primary years, and that, even then, they may not have mastered all that the Church teaches. Again, if you read through the sample in the Appendix, you can see that we have learned to give the parents the answers— enough so they are accurate in teaching their children, but not so much that they feel swamped by it all.

What do parents want for their children?

We know parents want to be involved with their children's faith. Many wish their own faith could be stronger. But in the life of faith, we know that nurturing and tending our faith experiences is vital. The Holy Spirit certainly works in our hearts, calling us to ever-deeper faith, but we must respond! Faith left unattended will grow dim, as a fire turns from flames to embers before it turns to ashes.

Modern parents are often very busy people, but they want to find a way to do this that fits into their modern lives. For them, much has become electronic while for the Church, much has not. Our "high touch" approach is welcome to many, but it must be well matched with a "high tech" approach to communications. This means more electronics, e-mail, Web sites, all in addition to in-person gatherings. We must be careful not to end personal meetings but also careful to enhance them with the modern means of communication and connection.

Parents actually tell us in parish after parish that they do want the help of a parish catechist to coach them to form their own children. They feel unequipped for this task. They lack self-confidence because they often lack a deep knowledge of the faith. For those who are away from the practice of their faith, many want to find a way to reconcile with the Church, but this reconciliation may not take place before their child is out of elementary school! We have to be ready to offer them support and a warm welcome *now*. If we wait until everything is perfect in their lives, we may never reach them. And the way we approach them must be with compassion, hope, mercy, and love.

What we need to succeed

The first thing needed in order to make this work is a clear, shared vision and belief that parents can and should play this vital role in their children's formation.

The second thing we need in order to succeed is a strong, well-written resource that serves as guide and text for all who are involved.

The Holy Spirit certainly works in our hearts, calling us to ever-deeper faith, but we must respond!

The third thing needed, of course, is to have the parents in the room with us. This calls on us to market well the invitation we make to them. This will be tricky because we're coaching them to do some things that are new to most of them: to help their children memorize certain prayers; to *model* the sacraments for their children by taking part themselves, as much as they are able based on their marriage situation, and if they are not able, to explain this to their children; to bring into the picture any non-Catholic or even non-Christian parents, guardians, or partners; to have certain sacramental items in their homes, such as holy water, prayer resources, sacred music, a sacred calendar of feasts and seasons, parish schedules of liturgies and formation events; to pray at all meals together; to pray at other times; and to *live* Catholic social teachings in a demonstrable way, allowing their children to learn by osmosis.

This requires a level of commitment on the part of the parents. We're raising the bar here and we have **great expectations** for them—greater than we have had in the recent past. To help formalize this and make it work, and to help parents really embrace the task given to them at the baptism of their child when he or she was "entrusted to their care," we will make clear that we expect parents to take their proper role in this effort.

....

PRINCIPLE TWO:
We can succeed only if we establish a loving and working bond between the household and the parish.

....

This leads us to Principle Two: We can succeed only if we form a true bond with each household, one of trust and love, one from which the parents feel empowered and trusted. Such a bond serves two important purposes. First, it helps parish leaders remember that, in the end, parents are indeed the ones primarily responsible for the formation of their own children. We must provide resources, opportunities, and coaching. Second, it helps parents remember this, too. They must commit themselves to do this with their own children, but with our support.

The terms of such a bond between households and the parish are, of course, two-sided: one side is on the part of the parish and the other is on the part of the household.

The role of the parish

This leads us to Principle Three, which is that any such process in which parents are being asked to form their own children, has a vital role for the parish to play. This is true because of our Catholic theology of what it means to be Church, but our common sense also leads us to it.

It's simply never enough, for example, to hold a meeting for the parents of second graders, give them a book on Eucharist, and send them home with the demand that they use this book to form their own children. Even actively engaged parents would find that difficult. For those who are inactive, they would find it nearly impossible.

....

PRINCIPLE THREE:
Any faith formation process you use must have a vital role for leaders of the parish to play.

....

It's never good to separate the household from the parish completely. The households in the parish must become *households of faith*, steeped in Catholic life and culture. This requires the presence and activity of the parents or guardians in the formation process. In the plan being presented here, the role of the catechist shifts from convening a class of children to coaching a group of parents-with-children for faith formation. The method is not to teach them what they need to know but by coaching parents to do that using the resource provided by the parish.

On the part of parish leaders, the truly most difficult part is that they will have to set aside their agenda, for example, to make sure the children understand transubstantiation before first Communion, or to make sure they are coming to Mass every week. Instead, they will have to focus on the needs and desires of those parents. They will have to help the parents take small steps toward deeper faith and deeper engagement. We know that the more we focus on the parents or guardians in this process, focus on their needs and their current situation in life, the more successful we will be in helping them grow in faith.

The role of the coach

So we want to *overlook the shortcomings of the parents* and focus on their strengths. We sometimes tend to find fault first but coaching requires us to actually build on their virtues and strengths. Our role as coach is not to judge others but to advocate for their potential. Great coaches expect others to bring all of their talents and energies to the task of forming their own children. They have great expectations for people and help them achieve them.

The ultimate goal is the development and greater engagement and participation of the whole household in the life of the church, both at the parish and in their homes as they develop households of faith. Parents are the *closest* ones to the children and play THE key role in forming them. This is true whether we like it or not. They live in the same house, or at least see each other with regularity. The example and words of the parents are naturally very formative.

Pastors, staff people, and catechetical leaders are ideally positioned to play the role of this sort of non-judgmental coach. They have the respect of the parents. They have the knowledge of the faith and can help parents pass that along to their children. And they can guide parents to take the steps needed for true reconciliation as they become ready. The eventual lifelong faith of their children literally depends upon this process.

The role of the catechist-coach, then, is to help the parent onto this road, and to help him or her accelerate the journey down it. How does coaching happen? There are key dimensions which flow directly from Catholic spirit and tradition. First, the coach establishes a real, warm and parent-centered relationship, where there is trust, honesty, and helpful advice. Second, the coach engages in specific and carefully planned training that enables the parent to take the lead in forming the child. And third, the relationship is positive and affirming between coach and parent—identifying what is best in them, and raising expectations. Instead of looking for problems to fix, we look for what's working in their household and build on that.

QUESTIONS FOR DISCUSSION

1. What would be the chief obstacles to organizing for such a program in your parish?

2. What outcomes can you foresee as a result of organizing to coach parents like this?

   For the children...

   For the parents....

   For their whole household and extended family...

   For the parish overall...

CHAPTER THREE

A plan to help children grow up Catholic

Growing up Catholic begins at baptism. This is the moment when the parish and the parents meet in a holy moment of celebration and initiation. In the words and actions of the rite of baptism itself, the message is clear: This child has been entrusted to the care of the parents. They are the ones primarily responsible for raising this child in faith. They are the ones who will model faith—or not—and set this child on a "faith course" that lasts a lifetime.

The insight and information, the skills and "faith habits" which they will need—these must all be learned. Who will teach this young couple how to create a household of faith, how to talk to their child both *about* God and *with* God? Who will help them teach their child the customs and lifestyle of the Catholic faith? Who will coach them to fill their home with sacred activities and objects, laced into daily life naturally and easily? Things like:

- Prayer before meals, at bedtime, and upon rising in the morning
- Observance of feasts and seasons of the year
- Seeing the events of life and the world through the lens of faith
- Forgiveness in abundance, seen as an act of faith
- Hospitality toward neighbors, friends, and even strangers
- A heart for the poor—a place for them in the family decisions about donating time or money
- Attendance at parish liturgies
- Family meal times where conversation is directed toward caring and interest in one another
- Sacred music and objects around the house

If their home is filled with these things, the

children raised there will be naturally inclined toward seeing them as important and essential to life.

Today's reality

But most young couples would not know how to create such a home unless they were coached to do so by someone. In previous generations, as we saw above, this coaching was done by the parents of the young couple or single parent. Faith was passed from generation to generation as each learned from the previous one how to pass on that faith. As we saw earlier in this book, the means by which this was done did not involve classes at the parishes in order to prepare for baptism. Rather, the household itself in combination with the parish was the place where formation occurred. Children formed in the faith and life of the Church (as just described) passed that on to their own children after they became parents themselves.

As we said above, there are two groups of these young couples or single parents. One group is in the class of families in the Church today where the faith does continue to be passed from generation to generation. They actually do have God-talk in their homes and other faith elements of many kinds. They are frequent participants in the liturgical and social life of the parish and their child or children will certainly be present with them at those times.

The other group (which is larger) is only marginally involved in parish life. Like the Church as a whole, these appear at our door-step mainly when need drives them to us: birth, death, marriage, crises of various kinds, or the holidays.

But today in this latter group, that passing on of the faith from generation to generation has slowed down and in many cases, it has stopped. We find ourselves in a downward cycle. How can parents create a household of faith unless they were tutored in how to do that by being raised in one themselves?

How can we reverse the downward cycle for this group, and help the young generation of parents who are currently on the margins of our parishes re-start this development of households of faith? How can we coach them to form their own children in faith?

It all begins at baptism

As we said earlier, this begins at baptism, during the preparation process which the parish requires young couples to complete before the baptism of their child.

What we often do right now is we require all young couples—whether active in parish life or not—to attend a baptism preparation process in our parish. We use preparation materials, most of which we buy from Catholic publishers, and which are usually quite good. These materials introduce the couple to the rite of baptism, and help them think about their role in the faith life of their new child. They may learn about the meaning of the symbols, the words used in the rite itself, the policies about who can or cannot serve as their child's baptismal sponsor or godparent, and so forth.

For the actively engaged group of young couples, this all makes sense and they take seriously what baptism means as well as their role in the faith life of their child. The current process is sufficient.

For the unengaged group of couples, the content of these sessions often does not have much meaning. For many, the process itself is a hoop through which they must jump in order to get their child baptized at the parish. They do it, but their main goal is get through it and get it behind them.

Often, one of these parents is not Catholic, and often neither is actively participating in the life of the parish. They may attend liturgy only now and then, rather than week in and week out. Their home may not have the "faith elements" described above in them at all. Their home and habits aren't faith-centered mainly because faith is not central to their lives.

Our expectations

Often, our expectations of the unengaged couple are not very high. We don't have **great expectations** but rather weak ones for them. Parish life is busy, we tell ourselves, so we don't have time to coach and nurture every couple. Besides, their lives are packed with mobile electronics, TV shows, jobs, friends, family, and

now this new baby. We often believe that our chance of winning them over to a fuller faith life is not very good.

So we go ahead and baptize their child and hope for the best. We are delighted to see them when they do take part in parish life and we welcome them warmly. But we know that when their child comes back to us to prepare for the

How can we coach parents
to form their own children in faith?

sacraments of penance and Communion, we and they will have a lot of catching up to do.

Another idea

One idea finding more and more acceptance in parishes today is to have a dual process for baptism preparation. One approach (Plan A) could be rather simple and would be aimed at those who are already attending Mass and participating in parish life. It could involve several sessions using published materials as a guide. For actively engaged couples, this may be more than adequate. (See the Parent Coaching Center on the Web site for more information and resources.)

The second approach (Plan B) would be aimed at the unengaged couples, and would have evangelization as its primary aim. In this second process, we take intentional steps to help this couple deepen their relationship with Christ and the Church.

We do this by inviting them into a retreat or retreat-like parish process through which they could have an encounter with Christ. This retreat might not be called a "retreat." (Most people don't identify retreats with fun activities! And the "fun factor" is very important to young couples or single parents. Therefore, even though throughout this resource, we use the term "retreat" you may wish to call it something else.) This retreat could happen right at the parish, on three consecutive meeting times, just as Plan A does. But the meetings would not merely follow the published materials for baptism prep. Rather, we add a new dimension to them, namely this retreat-like dimension of preparation. In this retreat-like prep process, the young couples or single parents would not only learn about, but also experience the Living Christ. They would have an encounter with Christ.

This retreat is designed to be used at the local parish level for parents who are in preparation for the baptism of their child. It will be especially effective for young couples or single parents whose relationship with the Church is tenuous or even non-existent. However, couples or single parents who are more deeply engaged with the parish would also benefit greatly from experiencing this retreat.

It may be used either before or after the baptism of their child or young adult. Many parishes will find Lent to be a good time to hold this retreat since it is during Lent that we prepare for baptism.

This retreat would also be a benefit to other adults in the parish who may wish to renew their faith and their baptismal promises. Adapted slightly, it would also be an excellent retreat for youth and young adults as they prepare for confirmation, which is also a sacrament of initiation.

The retreat is organized by leaders in the parish community and carried out entirely by them. Outlines are provided in the retreat notes (found on the Web site) for all the talks, prayer services, and handouts. The maximum number of new retreatants is about forty for any one occasion.

The best scheduling format is to hold the retreat on Thursday and Friday evening and Saturday morning, on three consecutive days. Keeping these three times as close together as possible is best for the flow of the retreat. This may not be possible because of people's busy schedules, but timing as close to this as possible will work best.

You might consider providing a parish fund to help pay for babysitting or child care for the period of the retreats to allow young couples with kids to be present. For some of them, the cost of babysitting for such a long period of time may be prohibitive. We do not suggest that the parish get involved with child care mainly due to safety issues and because, for the parents preparing for baptism, there will be many newborns.

We encourage you to invite non-Catholic spouses to attend with their Catholic partners.

Our hope is to help create a "household of faith" which is very difficult for one spouse if the other is not engaged at least a little. See below for notes on hospitality for non-Catholics at the time of sacramental celebrations.

What about learning the rites?

As we come to the end of the evangelization process, we can turn to the important work of reflecting on the rites themselves. Such reflection is indeed powerful and evangelizing in and of itself once the initial encounter with Christ has begun the journey of faith for them.

One example of an enjoyable retreat which can be done with as few as half a dozen volunteers is *I Claim You for Christ*, which is a reproducible resource found on our Web site. This retreat/marriage prep program occurs in three parts:

- On the first night, the team and participants trace their journey of faith since their own baptism, right up to the present. During this discussion, couples would be invited and coached to name the issues which may have kept them from a fuller participation in parish life. Without becoming a complaint session, this is a freeing moment for many couples to finally name the obstacles keeping them from participation.
  - » About 3-4 hours
  - » May include supper
  - » Parishes do not provide child care for these evenings because of all the newborns, but they do make a fund available for couples who need it to help each couple pay a babysitter of their choice.
  - » All the talks and discussions are fully outlined in the resource from the Web site, *I Claim You for Christ*.

- On the second night, which may be the following night, or a night in the following week, the team leads the group to understand and experience more fully the paschal mystery. This involves a presentation on what it means to "die in Christ," a discussion of their own experience of it, and the sacrament of penance.
  - » About 3-4 hours
  - » May include supper once again, during which the group would return in memory to the previous evening and share their thoughts about what happened
  - » Parishes may choose to use a form for the sacrament which allows the couples to celebrate forgiveness in a communal setting. This is recommended in the notes.
  - » At the end of this evening, a short celebration is held, which may include wine, sodas, and snacks.

- On the third night, the work turns to a covenant with the parish. In this process, the parish promises to provide coaching, resources, and support, plus a huge welcome to both spouses even if one is not Catholic. The couple likewise promises to form their child in the faith of the Church by naming specific things they will do to promote this.

» About 3-4 hours

» May include a meal once again

» This session may end with Eucharist. We warmly recommend that in the notes.

» The "covenants" should be in writing—all the materials for this are in the retreat notes—and may be presented to the couple later at the actual baptism of their child as a keepsake.

» Some couples may wish to continue to relate to their small group leader from this retreat, and they should make themselves available for this. An ongoing relationship will help insure the growth in faith of this household.

We could certainly invite those couples in the Plan A process to also attend this retreat, along with others from the parish. Its focus is not on baptism per se, but on conversion to deeper life in Christ. Who doesn't need that?

After baptism, what then?

After the baptism preparation retreat, it won't work to thank them for being there, say good bye, and hope they remain active in their faith. Instead, we must continue to coach them, offering them a relationship with the parish as a whole, and possibly with a specific individual or couple from the parish. This ongoing coaching might be done by family members or friends. Or the table leaders from the retreat may in some cases maintain contact with the young couples or single parents.

The resource needed for this period after the baptism of their child would be

- at least partly delivered via e-mail, Twitter, Facebook, or other social networking communications systems
- partly delivered in person by members of the *I Claim You for Christ* team
- and partly delivered via postal mail.

The resource designed for this period is called *Entrusted to Your Care* and it is available as an electronic resource on the Web site PastoralPlanning.com. In the rite of baptism

As their young child prepares for a significant moment in his or her faith journey, **we will coach the parent to take the primary role in forming the child for each specific step.**

the child is entrusted to the care of the parents. These resources help make that more real and intentional. They assist parish leaders in coaching young parents about what that means.

Once the child reaches early childhood, if these steps have been taken, both the child and the parents will have this basis to build on. Even if they remain only marginally connected to the parish during these years, we have provided them with memories and experiences to which they can return again and again.

Sacrament preparation is next

As the child reaches the early years of elementary school, we continue to coach the parents as the family prepares for first reconciliation (sometimes called first penance or confession) and first Eucharist (or first Communion).

This is the ideal time to expand the relationship begun with this young couple or single parent at baptism and in the years since baptism. Now is the time to offer them a true and deep partnership with the parish. As their young child prepares for a significant moment in his or her faith journey, we will coach the parent to take the primary role in forming the child for each specific step:

- Coming to understand what it means to "break the rules" or to act in unloving ways toward God, others, or even themselves.
- Understanding sin.
- Seeing the possibility of being forgiven by God endlessly and freely. But also the need to ritualize that and let it touch them deeply: confession and absolution.

- Experiencing the closeness of Christ in the Eucharist.
- Knowing the Holy Spirit lives within us, guiding and forming us constantly to pray, act with justice, and love.

So during these years of formation, why not use a resource through which you coach the parents to do all the formation needed to prepare for these sacraments? (The sample materials in the Appendix are from such a program.)

After the first sacraments

We often notice a decline in the number of students in the grades immediately following first penance and first Communion. Many parents stop sending their children to the parish for formation because they feel they have "done their duty" by making sure the child received these sacraments at least once.

But if you have coached them through the sacraments, gotten to know the parents (including any who are not Catholic), and set the stage for future engagement, then third, fourth, fifth grades and beyond is the time to continue the process! Here we need a real "Partnership with Parents" and this can come only through the parish itself.

Whole Family Formation. In Whole Family Formation, we proceed on two possible avenues. We call the first "Plan A: Learning Centers for Parents" and the second "Plan B: Whole Family Catechesis."

Plan A: Learning Centers for Parents. On the first avenue, we can offer parents a learning event which occurs while their children are in their regular religious education classes. For parents whose children are in the Catholic School, we suggest they gather at one of their regular parent meeting times, transforming it to become a learning event.

In Learning Centers for Parents, everyone begins in a large group with a very brief prayer, then all are offered a choice among several 15-20 minute learning centers. In each learning center, the parents get "hands on" training and are also given resources to take home and use there.

During the course of the event, each parent can attend two or three of the short small group sessions. Parents like this option because it moves along quickly, they get "just enough" to prime the pump for them, and in each learning center they receive resources to take home and use with their children.

Examples of learning center options include:

- ✒ **Three age-appropriate options:** Led by a trained teacher or other professional educator in the parish or community. We provide the outline and notes for these three options on our Web site. Each theme is explore with reference to
  » Children in pre-school or very early childhood
  » Children in the intermediate years after the first sacraments and up to middle school
  » Junior and senior high youth

- ✒ **A deeper look at the theology** of this topic, using the *Growing Faith* booklets which present the *Catechism* in plain English. A trained religion teacher, pastor, or pastoral staff member may lead this segment. We provide a resource for this on the Web site.

- ✒ **Seasonal activity learning**, such as for Advent, Lent or other key Feasts. You might have two or three such centers if you have enough people for them. We provide learning center resources on the Web site.

In this plan, the parish leader might set up five learning centers for the meeting. Each parent has time to choose two among them, unless the time allowed permits three. If they have one child in kindergarten and one in seventh grade, for example, they might choose two of the age appropriate centers. Or if they have one child in the program and no more, they may choose an age appropriate session plus one of the others.

The schedule for a meeting like this would run as follows. (Remember, the parents are normally doing this while their children are in the regular religious education session for the week, so we have only about fifty minutes, unless you schedule differently. The 6:30 PM starting time given here is arbitrary.)

6:30 PM Gather for prayer (five minutes)

6:35 PM Dismiss them to choose their first learning center

6:55 PM A five-minute break to move among learning centers

7:00 PM The second learning center session begins

7:20 PM Adjourn so the parent can meet their child

School program parents may attend at the same time as those from the parish religious ed program. Or you may schedule them at a regular time when school parents would otherwise be gathering, resulting in two different gatherings, one for school and one for parish religious education.

The theme for each event is taken directly from the basic text being used by the children in the parish. The basic themes of all the textbooks being used in the Church today include these ten topics. Notes to assist you in coaching parents are provided on the Web site for each of these.

- Revelation, Creation, and the Nature of God
- The Trinity
- The Person of Jesus Christ
- The Church: Its People and Mission
- Christian Morality and Living the Commandments
- The Sacraments and Liturgy
- The Kingdom of God and How We Are Called to Help Build It
- Scripture (which is also part of revelation)
- Christian Prayer
- Catholic Social Teaching

Plan B: Whole family catechesis. We can offer a series of events very similar to the ones used for the first sacraments in which parents-with-their-children attend and work together. Unlike the Learning Centers for Parents which we just described, where parents learn without their children present, during these events the children do spend part of the event with their parents.

In these, which can occur about once for every unit of the children's textbook, or less often in cases where this is more practical, parents are coached on how to talk with their children about the core beliefs of our faith, in age appropriate ways. We call these events by a name which defines them: Whole Family Catechesis.

What is a family? When we use the term family here, we are well aware that families today take many shapes. All types of families should certainly be welcome.

One commonly used schedule plan for Whole Family Catechesis is as follows. (Remember, the parents or guardians attend these meetings with their children. If they have both younger and older children, you will see below how we suggest you handle that.)

6:30 PM Gather for very brief prayer (five minutes)

6:35 PM Parents are coached to introduce their child or children to the topic for this meeting

6:40 PM Younger children are dismissed, just as in children's Liturgy of the Word. They process out with catechists to another room where they are offered a Scripture story, music, video, plays, or other exercises for twenty minutes. Adults and youth remain to explore the topic in greater depth, using a well-prepared resource to guide their learning.

7:05 PM The children return and the families work through an exercise to integrate what the parents and older children have just learned. A simple, brief, one- or two-item "household plan" emerges from this for the coming week. "Here's one thing we will do…" (The notes provided on the Web site help you develop this with the families.)

7:20 PM Wrap up, brief prayer, close with refreshments and sacred music playing—a fun and exciting ending.

Holding one Whole Family Catechesis session per unit of the children's textbook is the perfect plan. You can prepare parents for what the children will learn. For many parishes, however, it's only possible to hold two or three Whole Family Catechesis sessions per year. They may hold one as autumn programs begin, another near Advent, and another connected to Lent. We challenge all parishes to gradually increase the frequency of their Whole Family Catechesis sessions to reach a number which allows you to coach the parents about every key topic in the textbook.

In a later chapter we discuss how to prepare the resource for Whole Family Catechesis.

Junior and senior high

If parents have been coached to form their own children in faith from baptism up to early childhood, then through the first sacraments, and again in the key elementary years of school through learning centers and whole family catechesis, then coaching them to continue to form their junior and senior high children is the obvious next phase.

The Whole Family Catechesis and Learning Centers for Parents we just described will help prepare parents for this age level. But beyond that, we have created an exceptional process for bringing parents and their young adult children together in conversation about faith. The process is contained within the *Growing Faith* Mini-Courses, offered on the Web site. It's called **Learn and Teach**.

In Learn and Teach, participants all work in small groups of whatever size divides your total group best. Parents sit and work with their own children, but possibly in groups of two or three families.

- Assign a portion of each *Growing Faith* booklet or other resource to each small group.
- Invite them to Learn—read and share insights based on the discussion questions and method we provide in the FREE *study guide for each booklet.*
- Then ask them to Teach in the large group, using a three-step process:
  » Name the three or four (or more) major points learned in this segment and write them on a white or black board, or on flip chart paper.
  » Present them to the large group with explanation.
  » Choose one or two of these major points (the ones that seem most cen-

tral to faith) and create a question or exercise for discussion—participants may wish to use some of the suggested questions or exercises in the booklet or the study guide. Lead a conversation or exercise in the large group, using this discussion question and this method:

- Ask participants in the large group to work in pairs.
- Pose the question or exercise and invite the pairs to work together to respond.
- Invite each pair to briefly present its outcome to the large group.

※ Before going on, the leader may wish to make observations or summarize what happened in this segment.

We have prepared Learn and Teach segments on forty-eight key topics, covering every dimension of Catholic teaching as presented in the *Catechism of the Catholic Church*. Visit the Parent Coaching Center on the Web site for more information.

In conclusion, here are the key points from this chapter:

- ※ Children are entrusted to the care of their parents at baptism and parents have the primary role in forming them in faith.
- ※ We help parents do this by coaching them at each age and stage of a child's development.
- ※ We also help parents deepen their own faith, since that is what will be passed on to their child. We help them do this both while we coach them and in a retreat-like setting with others.
- ※ In this way, the parish carries out its primary role of evangelization and sets the stage for future generations of parents and their children.
- ※ We are raising our expectations of parents. We have great expectations for them!

CHAPTER FOUR

What coaching is and what it is not

Principle Four is based on the idea that, when thinking about how to approach a group of children, there really should be no such thing as "the whole second grade." There are only "individual second grade children." In other words, each child is a unique person, not merely part of some group. For each child, there is a unique and important personal history and current life situation in which faith formation is occurring. We cannot assume about one child what we may know about another.

The role of the school teacher or catechist in the parish is to know the children under his or her care, to know each of them and, in a certain way, to develop a faith formation plan for each child. Principle Four is that for the catechist (just as for the pastor or any other pastoral worker), all ministry happens in the context of a human relationship.

....

PRINCIPLE FOUR:
All ministry happens in the context of a human relationship.

....

We should keep this idea before us at all times. When we're tempted to "throw the rule book" at someone who missed a deadline or didn't complete a task, we must remember that the culture of each household is unique. And also, everyone is in *relationship* with us. This principle is rooted in the Gospels and is the whole point of the Incarnation. God is in relationship with each of us, calling us by name, forming us into community, yes, but one by one by one.

This is a reflection of the life of the Trinity, and not something we take lightly. It's at the core of our faith. We live in community, and

> Your relationship to families serves as both the model of faith for their own lives as well as the loving moment in which you can **guide them to accept greater responsibility for their own faith development.**

any time we treat people as "just another student" needing help, we fail this theology.

Likewise, Christ is experienced by us as the energy of Love. God's love for us and Christ's undying love for his Father. "God is love," the Scriptures remind us in 1 John 4:7–8. The deep communion and intimacy with Christ to which we are called is in fact a call to be in relationship with God at all times in our lives.

What does this mean for a religion teacher or catechist? It means two things.

First, never think of those children whom you teach as a single group, all having the same life experience and history. Always realize that each is unique and each sees you as a guide and mentor.

Second, to know the child you must know the parents. You aren't merely relating to eight or ten children (or more in a school class or parish religious ed program) but to each child and his or her parents or guardians. And this wider relationship is the one on which coaching parents is based.

In coaching, you, the catechist, are stepping into the life story of a family. Whatever their history and past mistakes or successes, at this particular moment you're leading them to a deeper response in faith and a deeper understanding of that faith. Your relationship to them serves as both the model of faith for their own lives (isn't this a huge responsibility?) as well as the loving moment in which you can guide them to accept greater responsibility for their own faith development.

You're their coach. The Holy Spirit actually does the work in the interior life of each person—and within you as well, but you are the one called to lead them gently to see the Spirit at work.

What coaching is NOT

As you work with the parents of your children, you'll begin to see more long-lasting results. But there are some dangers. Mixing yourself up in a dozen or more family situations could easily lead you to take on more than is possible for you as a teacher or catechist-coach. Here are some pitfalls to avoid.

Therapy

You are not the "family therapist." Although the process and results of coaching can be therapeutic, you don't and shouldn't get involved beyond your scope. If you spot problems they need to face as a family (such as anger, violence, or abuse) you should refer them to someone who could help more, such as the pastor, a family therapist, or someone else on the staff whose job it is to help.

Therapy typically focuses on healing the past where a certain level of healing can occur. But that is not the task of catechesis. Your task, in contrast, is to guide them to move *forward* in life in a closer relationship to Christ and the Church. You do this by helping them understand our teachings and grow in their ability to pray, celebrate the sacraments, and live a Christian life.

Teaching

Although you may be more of a content expert than many parents, you have to be careful not to spend your time *giving the answers*. Instead, as a coach, you want to help them *discover those answers* in a way that will stick with them. You're more a guide than a teacher, and you want the parents to teach their own children. By doing this, the lessons all go home—in the hearts of the parents and children.

A set of tools

Coaching is also not merely a set of tools that you give to people. Instead, in coaching, you use tools to demonstrate a pathway. As you demonstrate the use of prayer or Scripture or Church teaching, gradually the parents and children begin to pick up on how to do this for themselves. Once they get over the barrier of "I can't do this" and they arrive in the land of "Yes, I *can* do this," the tools you've shown them will last a lifetime.

Doing it for them

This is precisely what we want to stop doing. We want to stop replacing parents with others in the formation of their children, no matter how well-meaning the others are.

Skills needed for successful coaching

There are certain skills that you as a catechist-coach will develop as you learn how to be this ring leader. For each of these, we're giving an example or two here, and as you finish reading through each, we'd like you to pause for a moment and ask yourself, "Can I do this?"

SKILL #1

The ability to be present

Many times in parish ministry we get so concerned with schedules and details and microphones that, as people arrive, we aren't really being "present" to them. We're busy worrying about other things. The most important skill you need as a catechist-coach is to let go of the details and be fully present to the parents and children as they arrive. The more you can be present, the better you will be as a coach.

SOME HINTS

1. Try to get into their world as you meet them when they arrive for the session or when you talk to them on the phone between sessions. What happened for them today, right up to this minute? What did they have to rush through or leave behind in order to be here?

2. Ask about them, rather then telling about yourself. If you had problems getting ready, or if the copier broke down, don't mention it. Instead, inquire into their day and their needs.

3. Welcome them warmly, even if they aren't quite following the pathway you have laid out for them. Don't let your own dislike for them grow into you resisting them. You need a ton of patience for this, but you're receiving powerful gifts from the Holy Spirit.

YOUR RESPONSE

Can you do this? Rate yourself on the scale below.

1	2	3	4	5	6	7	8	9	10
not very able				quite able					absolutely able

What one dimension of this is most challenging to you?

The ability to focus on your goals

You might think that the primary goal of the first reconciliation preparation process is to make sure the child is ready for their initial confession. And surely that is the most immediate of goals. We do want each child to be well prepared for their first and all subsequent celebrations of each sacrament.

But there is a much larger goal, which a good coach must always keep in mind, and that is to help launch this child on a *lifelong journey of faith*. This larger goal, we know, can be achieved only if we also reinvigorate the faith of his or her parents in the process.

A third, less immediate goal, and one that the catechist him- or herself really cannot be responsible for, is to allow the sacramental preparation process to spread new energy across the whole parish community.

If we restrict ourselves only to the more immediate goal of preparing a child for his or her first confession, which is a fairly straightforward process, then we may miss out on the larger goal of providing formation that will last a lifetime.

SOME HINTS

1. Some of the parents of your children may not themselves have the larger goal in mind. They may wish to hurry through the sacramental preparation process, in order to "get it over with." Other parents will enter into this and love it. So you are the one who must keep the larger goal of a lifetime of faith before your own mind.

2. In each decision you make regarding a family situation or requirement for the program, ask yourself how this will indeed help meet your larger as well as your more immediate goals. Let the goals drive your decisions.

YOUR RESPONSE

Can you do this? Rate yourself on the scale below.

1	2	3	4	5	6	7	8	9	10
not very able				quite able					absolutely able

What one dimension of this is most challenging to you?

SKILL #3

The ability to ask good questions
—instead of giving all the answers

Giving unsolicited advice and intruding with "all the answers" is not only disempowering, it's unnecessary. Resist the temptation to "give them a fish"; instead, teach them how to fish for their own answers. If you do find a need to offer advice or to give answers, try to do it in a way that leaves the parents in that position of being the ones primarily doing the formation. Don't talk over their heads, or directly to their children, as though they aren't in the room. Try to use questions to surface growth and learning.

HINTS

1. When coaching others, use phrases such as
   - "I have an idea that you might find useful; mind if I check it out with you?"
   - "Why do you think the Church puts so much emphasis on reconciliation?"
   - "What are some of your own experiences of forgiveness and reconciliation?"
2. When working with non-Catholic parents, guardians, or partners, you may ask similar questions, rather than lecturing or explaining Catholic thinking:
   - "How does what you believe about reconciliation and forgiveness match what we teach as Catholics?"
   - "How would you take this teaching home with you and put it into practice there?"

YOUR RESPONSE
Can you do this? Rate yourself on the scale below.

1	2	3	4	5	6	7	8	9	10
not very able				quite able				absolutely able	

What one dimension of this is most challenging to you?

SKILL #4
The ability to ask for accountability,
but to also be very clear about your expectations

As a catechist-coach, you should never assume anything on the part of the parents. Back to those two groups again:

- Some parents will be ready and willing and will anticipate the work and be ready to roll when they come in the door. They'll never miss an event or session.
- Parents in the other group will get it wrong almost every time. They'll arrive late, or forget altogether. They'll have generally less overall commitment to this process.

But with both groups, your expectations should be clear. This is a strong skill for good coaching. And the expectation is that they will form their own children, not only for this sacrament, but for a lifetime of faith. For this reason, you also can expect them to develop and create a household of faith at home. The coaching notes suggest at-home activities and changes as part of the overall course.

HINTS

1. Treat each household group as a unique family. Don't assume for one group what you do for another. When you let them know what you expect, do so with their particular situation in mind.
2. This may result, for example, in you encouraging aunts, uncles, or grandparents to become involved in the formation process, if needed for that particular household.
3. When you announce your own expectations for attendance, participation, preparation, and at-home activities, do so with love and charity in your voice. If you sound demanding and near-critical, you will have less success as a coach. Remember, you aren't so much "getting them to do what you want them to" as "coaching them to want to grow in faith and share that at home."

YOUR RESPONSE

Can you do this? Rate yourself on the scale below.

1	2	3	4	5	6	7	8	9	10
not very able				quite able				absolutely able	

What one dimension of this is most challenging to you?

SKILL #5

The ability to give honest feedback

This skill is vital. It has two sides, and both are essential: First, never give fake praise to anyone. People can spot a phony from a mile away and once they stop believing you, you have greatly reduced your ability to coach them.

Second, never fail to praise. Your positive feedback as a coach is one of the chief things you bring to this process. Look for what it is about this person and their performance that's praise-worthy; be sincere, and generously encourage more positive behavior. The rule is "never fail to do this." No one should leave from your session without having been praised by you.

HINTS

1. Let their mistakes be their best teacher. If you see that they did not handle a situation well, give them honest feedback by offering constructive suggestions for improvement. For example, you might say something like this if a parent seems to avoid sharing about his or her own faith with their child. Word it as a suggestion and a question (see skill #3 above): "Frank, what do you remember about going to confession when you were in primary school? Share that with Johnnie."

2. Learn to gently confront areas that need attention using this method. Be careful not to make it sound like the parent or child is "bad" for missing a step, but be clear that each step should be taken.

YOUR RESPONSE

Can you do this? Rate yourself on the scale below.

1	2	3	4	5	6	7	8	9	10
not very able				quite able				absolutely able	

What one dimension of this is most challenging to you?

QUESTIONS FOR DISCUSSION

1. Look back at the descriptions of what coaching is and is not. What most excites you about partnering with parents as a coach rather than as a replacement for them in the catechetical process?

2. What skills for coaching do you already feel most comfortable or familiar with? How could you build on those to share this new way of forming parents and children with others?

CHAPTER FIVE

Getting started in your parish

One example of a resource to help you. The Appendix has an excellent example of a resource designed to coach parents in such a way that they are comfortable and happy passing on faith to their own children. Take a moment now to look this over. This is one lesson from the Growing Up Catholic first Eucharist (or Communion) preparation process. Note several things about this resource.

- The parent notes wrap around a reduced copy of the children's page. This allows the parents to see the child pages easily.

- The steps we ask the parents to take are numbered. This helps them follow a carefully planned process.

- Arrows direct the parents to various elements on the children's page.

- The parents are given all the answers to any questions, puzzles, or other activities. We never want to embarrass parents by

asking them to guide their child through an exercise that they themselves may not understand fully.

- The lesson is written at a reading level slightly above what would normally be suitable for a child. This allows the parent to become a real teacher, a needed guide through the lesson. Otherwise, the parent may feel unnecessary in the process.

- Many times throughout the lesson, the parent is asked to make sure the child understands the vocabulary and meaning of the teachings or prayers. This allows the parent to follow up with the child after the session at home.

- Every lesson includes a segment on the rites of the Church's liturgies.

- We always end by sending home a project, with clear instructions. By sending this home with both the child and parent, we hope one will call the other to the task.

- The parent notes and child pages are both in handout form, rather than book form. Handouts are more user-friendly. They tend to be taken home, especially after the parents and children work on them together. They are less intimidating and less expensive than whole books full of lessons. They can be posted to your Web site and made available to parents who may not be living together any longer. (Often in these cases, we want both parents to be involved, especially if the child lives part-time with each.)

It helps a great deal if the parish or school leader can put this resource into the hands of the parent or guardian a few days before the actual lesson. This gives them time to review it and prepare for "class." These lessons are provided in PDF format, which would also allow a parish to post them to a specific area of the parish Web site.

GrowingUpCatholic.com also contains these lessons, along with a wide range of other resources for parents—prayers to memorize, Catholic customs, background articles from *The Catechism*, and other elements.

Once you start using this approach, you'll never return to one that fails to include and coach the parents.

Your elementary curriculum outside of sacrament preparation

We have just shown you how a parent coaching resource works for sacrament preparation. Beginning to coach parents in this year of a child's life is essential. If we can guide these parents to be involved in these important turning points, we have a chance of keeping them involved in the following years.

Once you start using this approach, you'll never return to one that fails to include and coach the parents.

As we said already in Chapter Three, a parish organized to coach parents really begins the process at baptism and in the years immediately afterward. This sets the stage for sacramental preparation, where coaching parents is the obvious choice.

But what about third grade? What happens in the year after first confession and first Holy Communion? How can we be ready to "keep the ball rolling" with the parents who have tasted the success of working with their child for the sacraments?

For most parishes, it may be possible to invite the parents in the year after first Communion to one event per unit of the children's elementary book. This is possible in both the parish and school programs. But, while coaching for the sacraments was heavy on detail and specific Catholic culture and practices, it's probably most practical in the following year to help parents and children become conversant in more general areas of belief and practice. A possible plan might look like this:

- It may not work to convert your entire elementary program to coaching in the same year. Begin small and grow the coaching elements. In some smaller parishes, of course, there is more flexibility, and a complete coaching program may be developed more quickly.

- Once you have worked with children and parents in second grade for the sacraments, plan to invite them back the following year for one coaching session at the beginning of every unit of the elementary textbook, or as often as possible—as described in Chapter Three. This would add only the parents of third graders to your coaching group, and those parents have the experience of the previous year. It would add five to seven events for the year of their child's third grade religion program.

Getting started in your parish

1. Form a committee, including the pastor, other staff, key volunteers, and some parents. Read and study this pastoral guide together, working through each section in dialogue with each other. Your initial committee should deal with these issues before finishing its work:

- Do you feel you have the needed leadership to organize and promote this in the parish?

- Do you have the catechists who can work as coaches? Many times, the coach you find will be someone who did not previously work in the children's program. Rather it may be someone from the RCIA or other adult formation ministry, because most of the coaching is aimed at adults, not children.

- Can you fit large groups of parents and children into your current facility? Do you need to rent space elsewhere?

- Partnering with parents this way has a minimal impact on your budget, but are there resources with which to purchase the needed parent "texts"? It is necessary to send them home with a solid resource to help deepen their understanding.

2. After a while, gather a larger group of parents, catechists, and leaders. Share the vision and process with everyone.

- In doing this, questions are sure to arise for which you may not have a ready answer. Anytime you shift from one method to another, such unseen matters will arise. Do not be blown off course by such questions. Welcome them as part of how you will plan well to succeed at partnering with parents in the formation of their children.

3. At some point, reach a decision together with the consent of the pastor and school or religious ed leaders.

4. Write up a simple plan with a timetable with dates, rooms, budget needs, and so forth—work with the annual parish calendar manager to secure the space and people you need.

- Look forward with your plan to expand this process beyond sacrament prep into the rest of your elementary program, confirmation preparation, or other formation processes.
- Think in terms of a long-range, ten-year plan such as the one pictured below. Plan to build slowly a parish and school religious education program that includes the parents as often as possible.

TEN-YEAR PLAN
You've got to start somewhere!

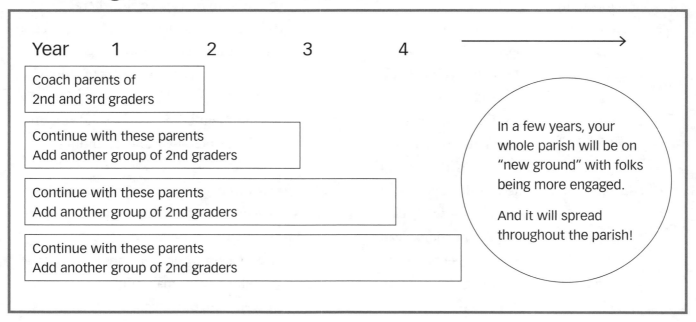

Year 1 2 3 4 →

Coach parents of 2nd and 3rd graders

Continue with these parents
Add another group of 2nd graders

Continue with these parents
Add another group of 2nd graders

Continue with these parents
Add another group of 2nd graders

In a few years, your whole parish will be on "new ground" with folks being more engaged.

And it will spread throughout the parish!

APPENDIX

Sample parent coaching notes

5 We Receive Holy Communion

We are going to receive our first Holy Communion

This is a very exciting time for us!

We Receive Holy Communion

➢ Catholics believe that Jesus **is really present** under the signs of Bread and Wine
➢ We share Jesus in Holy Communion
➢ We become a closer **church family**
➢ Jesus wants to come to us
➢ The Mass reminds us that Jesus died for us

We are the People of God!

1 In this lesson, your child will begin the **final period of preparation** for his or her first Communion.

2 Take the time after this lesson or during the coming week to go with your child to **visit the Blessed Sacrament** in your parish church. Make sure your child understands that Jesus is present there.

3 Teach him or her to talk with Jesus in personal ways, like sharing with a friend. In preparing for Communion, this will help create a strong sense of reverence for your child.

4 Make sure your child knows and gradually comes to believe that **Jesus becomes sacramentally present in the bread and wine** at Mass. It is his Body and Blood. All of us who take part in the Eucharist likewise become ever more the Body of Christ, one body and one spirit in Christ.

5 It is not too early to introduce this big word to your child: **Transubstantiation**. It is the word used by the Church to define what happens at Mass. There is no need to dwell on this at length with your child, but it is good to be aware of this term. To read more about this, see the *Catechism* articles 1373-1381.

6 Explain to your child that the Eucharist and our gathering on Sundays for Mass is the highpoint of all the Sacraments. It is that from which our whole Christian life flows each week - and that toward which we aim ourselves every week.

**Prayer Celebration:
Growing up Catholic means we
Gather with God's People**

A Prayer to Prepare Ourselves
for Holy Communion

Everyone begins by making the Sign of the Cross
In the name of the Father, and of the Son, and of the Holy Spirit. Amen.

Leader: Jesus, we believe in you and love you.
All: Make us ready to receive you in Holy Communion.

Leader: Jesus, thank you for loving us with your whole life.
All: Make us ready to receive you in Holy Communion.

Leader: Jesus, help us to be strong friends of yours.
All: Make us ready to receive you in Holy Communion.

Please listen to the Reader now.
Reader: A reading from the Letter of Paul to the Corinthians (1 Cor
11:26-28)
(At the end of the reading:) This is the Gospel of the Lord
All: Praise to you, Lord Jesus Christ!

Please listen to the leader.
When the time comes, please bring up your slip of paper with your promise to Jesus
written on it. Place it here on this table.

Let us pray together
(please pause after each line)

Oh Jesus, we are preparing to receive you
    in Holy Communion.
Help us to be loving and kind,
    help us to receive you
    and believe in you
    and love you with all our hearts.
We pray through Christ, our Lord. Amen.

Parent lesson plans for page two of the 5th lesson.
Follow the numbers.

1 Pray this with your child, helping them find their way through it as the leader guides you.

When the time comes, help them choose and write **the one special way they will prepare themselves for Holy Communion.** You should also choose and write one way that YOU will prepare yourself, and please share that with your child.

These might include things like:
  ➢ having a special intention in your heart when you come to Mass,
  ➢ asking Jesus to help you,
  ➢ being sorry for any sins,
  ➢ saying a special prayer,
  ➢ fasting,
  ➢ giving money for good causes

2 Making peace at home.

Many times, family life can be tough! Even in the most loving homes, there are quarrels and fights, people act selfishly or are even mean to each other. The preparation that we do for Mass leads us to seek peace in our homes. The road to peace is paved with

- Saying we're sorry when we hurt each other
- Accepting each others' apologies
- Giving each other signs of love such as notes, cards, little gifts, and hugs
- Admitting when we're wrong
- Being "the big one" in situations where fighting just makes things worse
- Praying for one another often
- Praying together at certain times of day
- Having signs of faith around the house

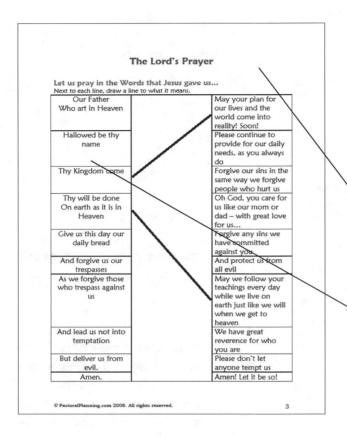

Parent lesson plans for pages 3 & 4 of the 5th lesson.
Follow the numbers.

1 This exercise may be difficult for younger children, but with your help, they will be able to work through it and **understand the Our Father much better.**

2 First, read through the words of the Our Father with them. We have provided you with **notes on the following pages** to help you. Use them but don't read them to your child.

3 Then help them find the correct meaning of each phrase of this prayer. Draw a line to that. We have given you two clues to get you started. Here's the key:

1 = 4
2 = 8
3 = 1 (given)
4 = 7 (given)
5 = 2
6 = 5
7 = 3
8 = 9
9 = 6
10=10

4 Work through this page with your child, helping him or her understand why **making peace** is part of the preparation for Communion. (The explanation is in the bottom section of this page.)

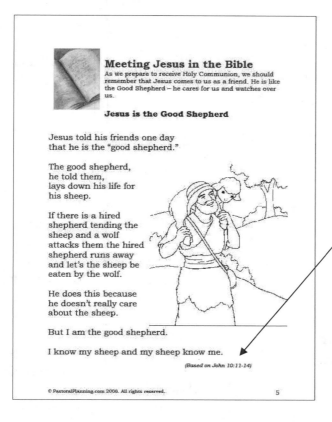

Parent lesson plans for pages 5 & 6 of the 5th lesson.
Follow the numbers.

1 We will now read about how Jesus is our friend, just as a shepherd is to his sheep. Begin by showing your child a **Bible.** Open it to show them this passage.

2 Tell them that we are going to read this story in words that we understand better.

3 Then close the Bible and ask them to read this passage aloud. Help them when needed. Ask your child to retell this story in his or her own words.

4 Time for a break! Help your child **enjoy** coloring this image of Jesus and the children.

Coloring time is a good time to be close to your child without necessarily talking about faith.

Don't be afraid to **put your arm around your child** during this time.

5 Your child may not be familiar with what shepherds do. Explain that they look after their sheep with **tenderness and love**. Jesus watches over us that way.

Parent lesson plans
for pages 7 & 8 of
the 5th lesson.
Follow the numbers.

The Sacrament of The Eucharist
Holy Communion

The Lord's Prayer

➢ Jesus teaches us how to pray
➢ At Mass, we pray the Our Father with words that Jesus taught us
➢ What do the words mean?

The Lamb of God
Practice this part of the Mass:

Lamb of God, you take away the sins of the world, **have mercy on us.**
Lamb of God, you take away the sins of the world, **have mercy on us.**
Lamb of God, you take away the sins of the world, **grant us peace.**

Holy Communion

The Priest or person sharing Communion says:
The Body of Christ

We say: **Amen!**

At home this week
Work on this together at home as a way of continuing the process of preparing for The Sacrament of The Eucharist

A plan for love.
Tell or draw one way you will be kind and loving this week.

With your parents	At school	With your friends	With Jesus in prayer

Rehearsal for Holy Communion.
You can receive Communion in two ways:

In your hand
Open your hands like a small bowl. Bow in reverence and hold your hands upward toward the priest or person sharing Communion. Say "Amen" when you are offered the Host. When handed the host, place it in your mouth immediately and swallow.

On your tongue
Bow in reverence and say "Amen" when you are offered the Host. Hold your head back just a little. Open your mouth and place your tongue on your lower lip until you feel the Host being placed there. Close your mouth and swallow immediately.

The chalice
Take the chalice when offered to you and drink a small sip.

1 Throughout these lessons, we have been learning about the parts of the Mass. You may wish to return to pages 3-6 of lesson one to review it one more time.

2 We have already treated the meaning of the **Our Father** in this lesson.

3 Help your child understand why we pray for mercy in the **Lamb of God**. Mercy, you can explain, is when God "looks the other way" when we sin. God endlessly forgives us, even if we don't really deserve forgiveness all the time. That's how much God loves us!

We pray for mercy, not because God withholds it, but because the prayer reminds us that we depend on God.

4 As part of the preparation for Communion, help your child **create a little plan** to be ever more loving in daily life.

5 This week, **rehearse** the reception of Communion with your child. Use the notes on the bottom of this page to help you. Your child will feel more comfortable if they are well rehearsed.

Additional coaching resources

Coach parents before baptism

Baptism is where the journey of growing up Catholic begins both for parents and for their child.

God's Own Child

BILL AND PATTY COLEMAN

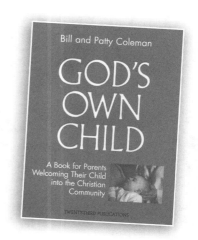

God's Own Child provides a way for you to begin the process of growing up Catholic in each child's life. Parents are coached to talk together, or with a friend, about the meaning of faith in their lives and how they will pass that on to their child. This is an appealing, proven, hands-on, adaptable resource to help you coach parents as they prepare for the baptism of their child. It works equally well for parents who are newcomers, returning Catholics, or regular parishioners. It is easy to use and can be incorporated easily into existing parish schedules. A *Leader's Guide* is also available.

Coach parents after baptism

After baptism the process of growing up Catholic is in the hands of the parents or guardians.

Entrusted to Your Care

LEISA ANSLINGER

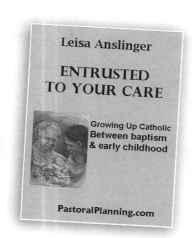

Using letters, e-mail, and personal contact, *Entrusted to Your Care* will help you implement a "bridge between baptism and early childhood." Well tested and creatively developed, these clever resources are aimed at busy young parents who may or may not be active in parish life themselves. Supported by a strong web site, this resource will prepare both child and parents for first penance and first Communion.

Coach parents to prepare their child for the sacraments

On Our Way with Jesus—*the best available sacrament preparation for children, families, and catechists!*

We Prepare for Reconciliation

FRANCOISE DARCY-BERUBE AND JOHN-PAUL BERUBE

We Share in the Eucharist

FRANCOISE DARCY-BERUBE AND JOHN-PAUL BERUBE

This exceptional program invites children, parents, catechists, and teachers to enter the mysteries of the faith more deeply, to pray more often, and to experience the sacraments of reconciliation and Eucharist as encounters with Jesus Christ.

Each child's book includes a FREE full-color 16-page insert that coaches the parents on their role in the preparation process. These guides offer parents encouragement and basic tips for sharing faith with their children. They also include morning and evening prayer cards for parents to share with their child.

NEW EDITION HIGHLIGHTS

- Delightful new design, built around color-coded, easy-to-follow themes
- New, easy-to-hold size for children
- Beautiful, all new, contemporary illustrations and photos throughout
- "What Have You Learned?" page at the end of each theme
- Recent changes in the liturgy from the Roman Missal
- "My Prayer Book" in the child's Eucharist book to cut out and assemble for prayer
- New Leader's Guides incorporate the child's book pages with each instructional page
- Imprimatur

Coach parents at the time of first penance and first Communion

The pedagogy here is called "Learn and Teach" in which young people learn the material well enough to teach it to their peers.

Growing Up Catholic is a carefully tested and well-crafted formation process designed for use within the parish or in home schooling. It provides the immediate preparation for first reconciliation, confirmation-in-restored-order, and first Communion. But it does far more than merely prepare a child for these sacraments. It also prepares children and their parents for a lifelong journey of faith as Catholics. And it does so in a way that is enjoyable, easy to do, and powerfully effective.

Growing Up Catholic
First Penance

GROWING UP CATHOLIC
First Penance (Reconciliation)

This is a complete system for coaching parents to form their own children in preparation for celebrating penance for the first time. Parents meet at the parish with their child, sharing in a parish event with other parents with children.

GROWING UP CATHOLIC
Confirmation in restored order

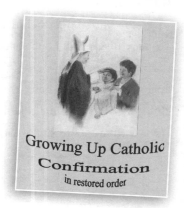

Growing Up Catholic
Confirmation
in restored order

If your diocese is one in which confirmation is celebrated before first Communion, then this is the resource for you. Connecting confirmation with Eucharist, this preparation process is hailed as the perfect way to help parents form their own children.

GROWING UP CATHOLIC
First Communion (Eucharist)

Growing Up Catholic
First Communion

Initiation is concluded when the child begins receiving Holy Communion. Like the two above, this process is one in which parents are coached to form their own children for this key moment, making it formation that lasts a lifetime!